HOW A LOG CABIN IS BUILT

Engineering Books for Kids
Children's Engineering Books

BABY PROFESSOR
EDUCATION KIDS

Speedy Publishing LLC

40 E. Main St. #1156

Newark, DE 19711

www.speedypublishing.com

Copyright 2017

A dwelling that is constructed using logs in known as a log cabin. They date back to Europe's ancient history, and in America they are typically associated with homes constructed by its early settlers. In this book, you will be learning how our early settlers built a log cabin as well as how to build a log cabin with today's resources.

AMERICA'S PIONEERS

Once they arrived on their new land, one of the first things the pioneers had to do was to build a place for their families to live in. If they were lucky enough to be surrounded by trees, they could construct a log cabin.

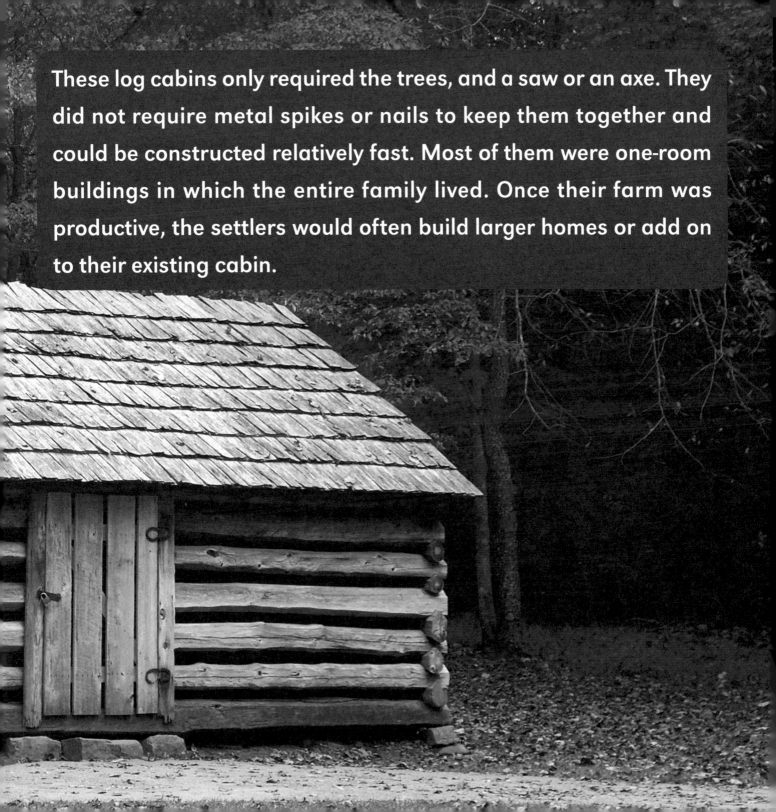

These log cabins only required the trees, and a saw or an axe. They did not require metal spikes or nails to keep them together and could be constructed relatively fast. Most of them were one-room buildings in which the entire family lived. Once their farm was productive, the settlers would often build larger homes or add on to their existing cabin.

CLEARING THE LAND

The early settlers would first have to clear an area of land where they wanted to build the house. They would want to include space surrounding the cabin where they would be able to plant a garden, construct a barn, and have some animals, such as chickens. They sometimes would have to cut trees down and remove the stumps. These trees would then be used in construction of the log cabin.

CUTTING LOGS

Once the land was cleared, they would have to cut the trees down to supply the logs needed to build their cabin. The trees would have to have straight trunks which made good logs for building their homes.

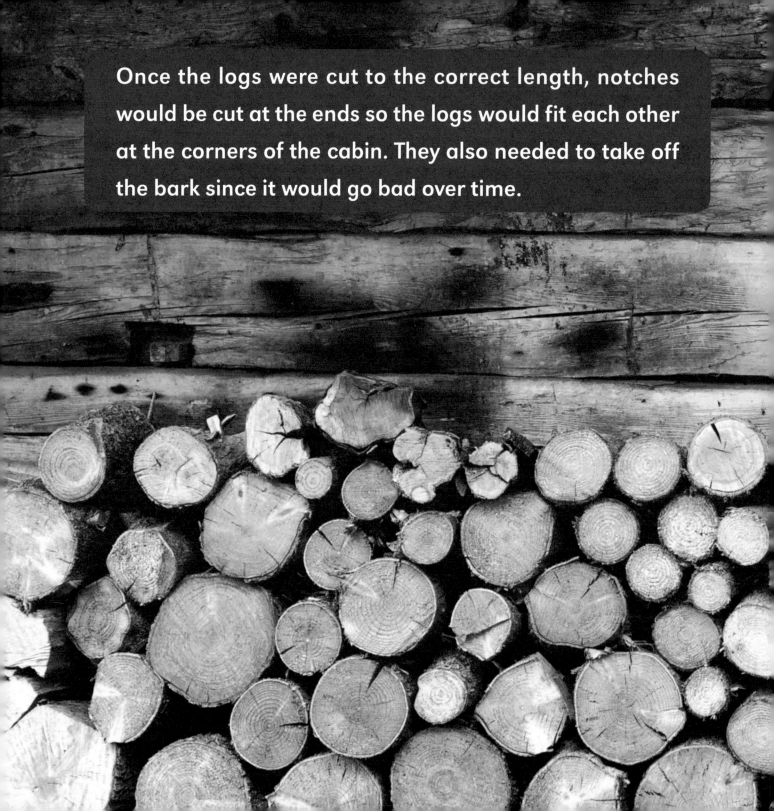

Once the logs were cut to the correct length, notches would be cut at the ends so the logs would fit each other at the corners of the cabin. They also needed to take off the bark since it would go bad over time.

CONSTRUCTING THE WALLS

All four of the walls would be built using one log at a time. If there was only one person building it, the cabin would typically only be six or seven feet tall since he could only raise the log that high. If he had assistance, the walls could be somewhat taller.

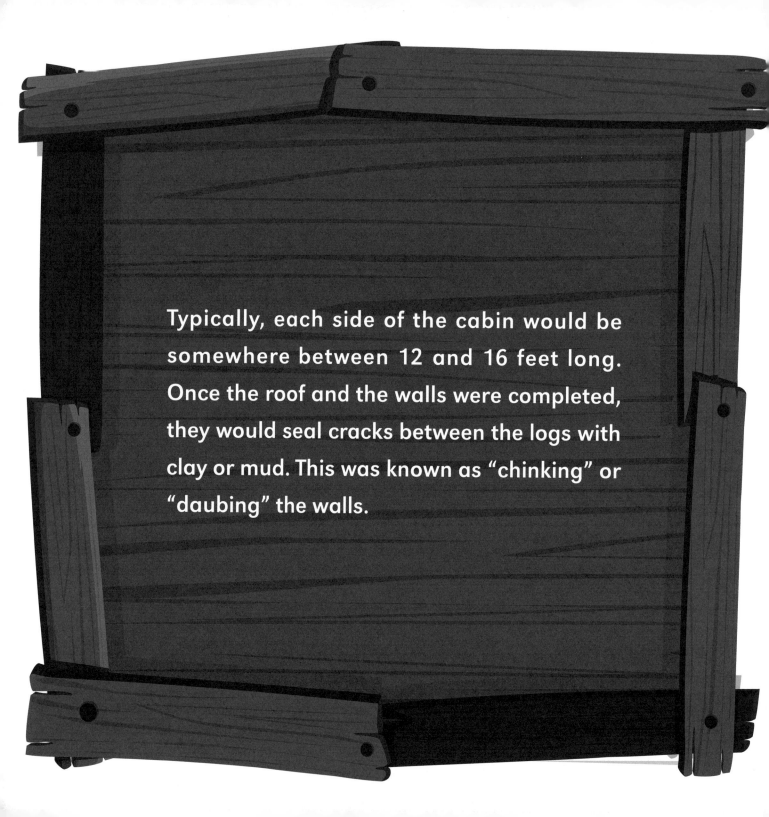

Typically, each side of the cabin would be somewhere between 12 and 16 feet long. Once the roof and the walls were completed, they would seal cracks between the logs with clay or mud. This was known as "chinking" or "daubing" the walls.

FINISHING TOUCHES

At one end of the cabin they would build a stone fireplace for keeping their family warm during the colder months as well as providing them with fire to cook with. Typically, there might be one or two windows for light, but glass was seldom available to them. They would often use greased paper as window coverings. The floors usually consisted of packed earth, but occasionally they might be made of split logs.

FURNITURE

When they would first move into their cabin, they typically did not have much furniture, other than one or two chairs, a bed, and a small table. Sometimes they had a chest they had brought from their homeland. In the chest, they would bring some other decorations, such as candlesticks or a rug to make their new cabin seem like home.

There are not very many older log cabins still existing since they were not built to be permanent dwellings. When the English settlers arrived in America, they would often build a more traditional home and convert the log cabins to be outbuildings used as sheds or shelters for animals.

BUILDING A LOG CABIN WITH TODAY'S RESOURCES

Today, most log cabins are constructed with many of the conveniences of the modern home. In fact, many people prefer them over the modern home because of their natural beauty and their rustic charm. As people got better at constructing log cabins, they created better tools to use in building the cabins. With the use of these better tools, a new log cabin could be built within only a few days.

Log Cabin Interior

THE FOUNDATION

The first step when building a log cabin is to set your foundation. The foundation must be able to carry the load and weight of the cabin. The foundation is used to move the cabin load into the sub-ground in a safe manner.

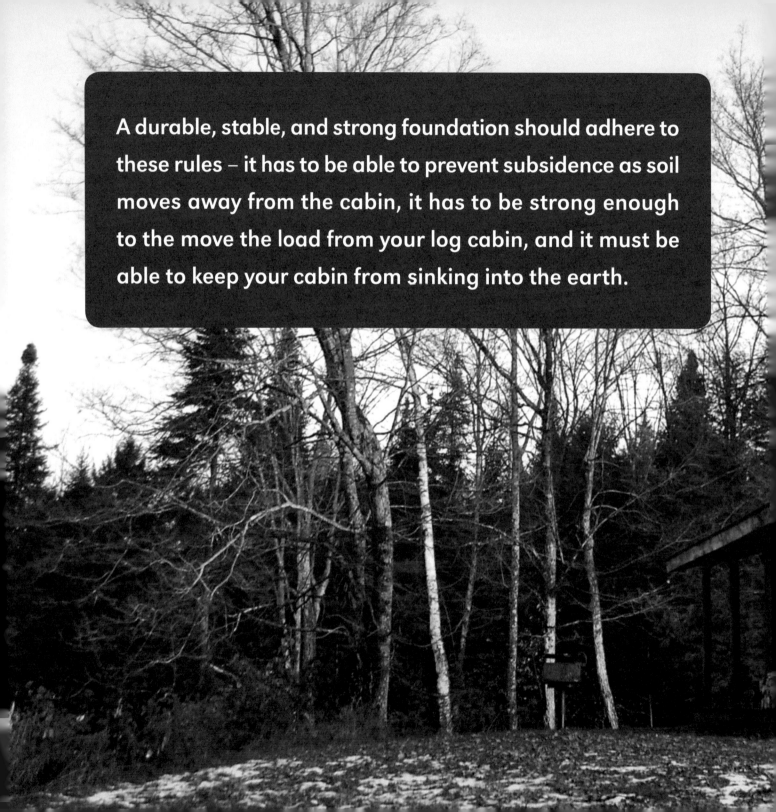

A durable, stable, and strong foundation should adhere to these rules – it has to be able to prevent subsidence as soil moves away from the cabin, it has to be strong enough to the move the load from your log cabin, and it must be able to keep your cabin from sinking into the earth.

NOTCHES

So far, it's probably not looking much like a log cabin, but all that will change once you start laying the logs. Prior to laying your logs, you will need to make a decision about what notching system you want to use for the corners of your log cabins. Remember when we discussed the notching of the logs in the earlier section?

There was only one way that it was done. The Butt and Pass notch is the favorite for modern cabin construction. This technique was recently invented to be easy for novices building their log cabins. Other types of notches include Full Scribed (Traditional), Full or Half-Dovetail, and Corner Post. Once the foundation has been set and you have decided what type of notch you will be using, the first set of logs are ready to be laid.

Full Dovetail

THE FIRST FOUR LOGS

Using your best cut logs, you will want to set your sill logs into the foundation you laid. Setting the logs into the foundation is typically done by using the best logs you cut. Once they are pre-drilled and cut to length you can lift these logs into position. You will then fix these logs together with short rebar pins. The perimeter of your cabin is now fitted.

FLOOR INSTALLATION

The floors of logs cabins usually are quite easy and fast to assemble since their construction consists of a suspended lumbar floor. You will need to notch the logs you just set so that the floor joists can be inserted. Make sure that the notch has the same width as the floor joist to create a snug fit with the floor joist. The final step is to plank the floor at right angles.

Log Cabin Floor and Interior

CONSTRUCTION OF THE LOG WALLS

Build the log cabin as if it does not have windows, openings, or doors. Keep stacking the logs until all four walls are up. For each layer of the cabin, you will want to turn the direction of each log. This will ensure that the wall remains somewhat level because of the natural taper of the log. If you are using the Butt and Pass notch type, you will be using short rebar fixings for fixing each log. In the alternative, you will need to scribe each notch and then you can stack them.

THE WINDOWS AND DOORS

To create the window and door openings, you will simply remove the lumber where you want the opening, supporting with a log and tacking cleats to sustain the opening.

ROOFING THE CABIN

Since most cabins are either rectangle or square, it should not be too difficult to roof it. If you want a traditional classic log cabin roof, you will want to build a pitched roof for your cabin.

There are typically four types of finish for a log cabin roof: thatched roof, traditional wood shingles, roofing felt, and metal sheeting. Once you have decided the finish for the roof of your cabin and placed the material on the gables of the roof, you have finished roofing your cabin.

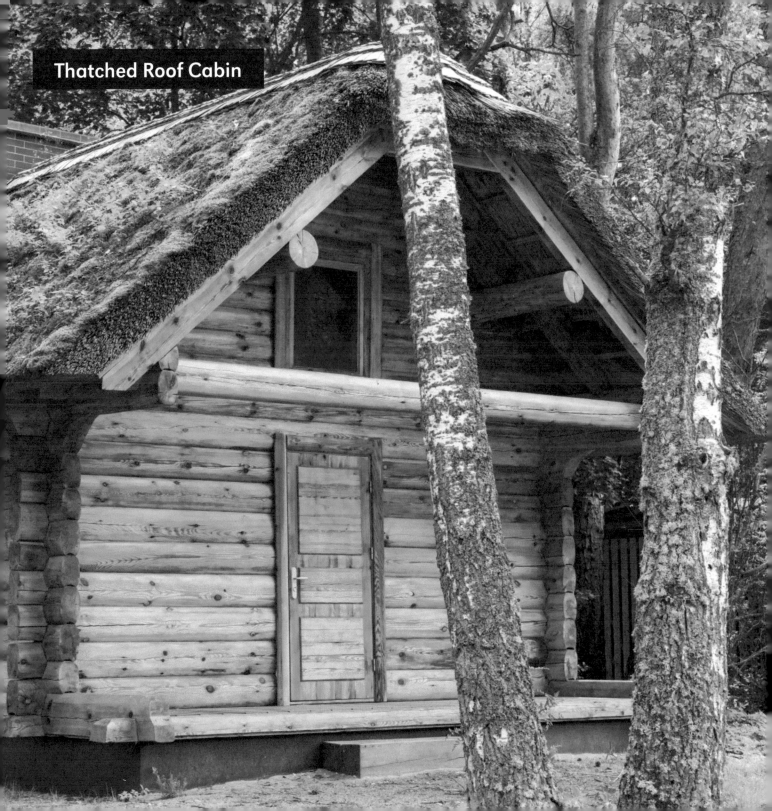

Thatched Roof Cabin

WEATHERPROOFING

Once you have built your log cabin, the final stage is to weatherproof it. Dampness in colder climates and moisture in humid climates can quickly damage your log cabin if you do not weatherproof it. The three most important factors when weatherproofing your home are cleaning, chinking, and staining it.

CLEANING THE LOGS

The first thing you want to do is clean your logs as they probably have collected dirt from the construction site or during transport. In addition, washing the logs will remove pollen, dust, and deposits.

Moisten the logs with water, then take a soft bristle brush, using a mild detergent, and scrub in small circles starting at the bottom of the cabin moving up to the top. Repeat the process, moving from the top of the cabin to the bottom. The cabin will need at least two days drying time.

STAINING THE LOGS

Once the bark has been removed from the logs you can typically apply a borate solution for protection. Once the cabin has been constructed, you can stain the logs to retain the logs' original color and protect it from the UV rays of the sun. The first time you stain your log cabin, the stain will last about 18 to 24 months, depending upon its exposure to UV rays.

Chinked Log Cabin Wall

CHINKING THE CABIN

Chinking is a log sealant that prevents moisture and air infiltration. You will definitely need to chink your log cabin if you used the butt and pass notch technique.

Any split, or crack, over 2 cm will need to be sealed and filled with chinking. You will apply the chinking, using a trowel, along the length of the joints in the logs. Use a damp cloth for cleanup and giving it a nice finish.

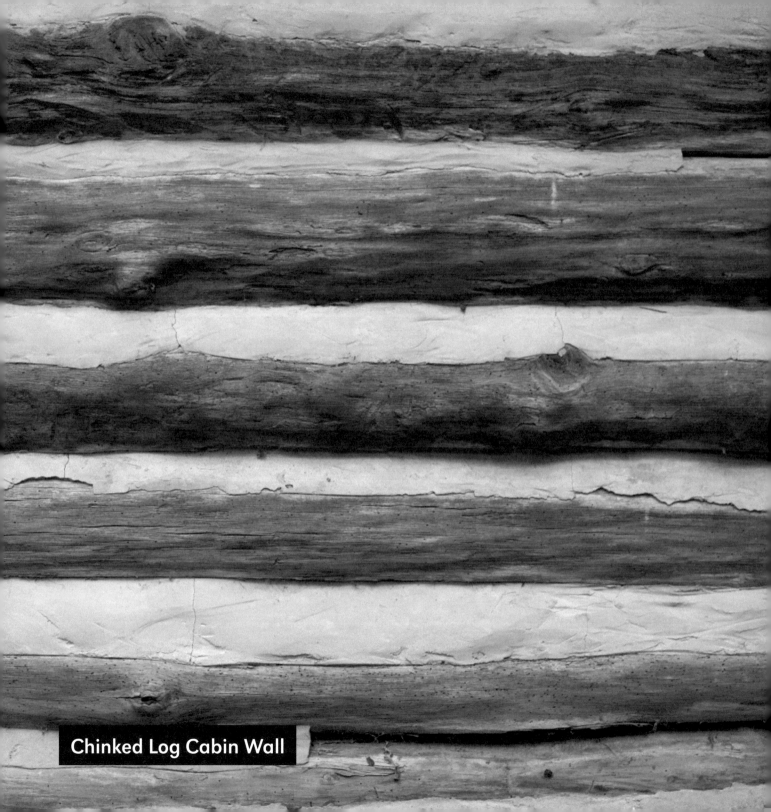

Chinked Log Cabin Wall

Your basic log cabin is now complete and ready for you to finish and decorate however you like. While it might seem more difficult to build than the early log cabins, with the manpower and tools available now, they are easier to build and built to last.

For additional information about how to build a log cabin, you can visit your local library, research the internet, and ask questions of your teachers, family, and friends.

Visit

BABY PROFESSOR
EDUCATION KIDS

www.BabyProfessorBooks.com
to download Free Baby Professor eBooks
and view our catalog of new and exciting
Children's Books

Made in the USA
Columbia, SC
12 January 2024